Dog Walking Weather

Dog Walking Weather

copyright Jack Wolf, 2022

front cover image Jack Wolf, 2021

The right of Jack Wolf to be identified as author or this work has been asserted by them in accordance with the copyrights, Designs and Patents Act of 1988. All rights reserved.

No part of this book may be used or reproduced in any manner whatsoever without the prior written permission of both the publisher and the copyright owner.

First Edition 2022

ISBN 978-1-7396972-1-1

published by Aurochs Underground Press, Bath, UK

Jack Wolf

Dog Walking Weather

Contents:

Flystrike	6
Behemot	7
Proustian Heifers	9
Fragments	10
Wired	11
Of Rats and Men	12
Rough Tor, with Waterloo and Sheep	15
Accidental Blue	16
Deviock Cross	17
Woodpeckers	19
Pink Sheep	22
Army Manoeuvres	23
Mont Blanc and the Virus	24
Lifeboats	26
Stoney Littleton Long Barrow, at Halloween	28
Managed Retreat	34
Equinoctial Horses	36
Everything is Connected to Everybody Else	40
Gnats Uprising in February	44
Hineni	45

Dog Walking Weather

Flystrike

Today I'll go

to the cold upland beyond Sibleyback
to the open land where feral ponies
congregate and sheep wear their tails long.
No risk of fly-strike here. Today, no fear
of fog. The rain-white stones
sparkle in the grey fuzz of the dawn

where thirty thousand years ago, the wind
here, where the land is highest, here
where sky is heavy as a press,
carved cheesewrings out of granite,
and wrung water from the stark
fruit land, the stacked circles of stone,

bearing bright nuggets of casserite, white tin.
Now all the seams are all worked out, the copper
  engine house
Wheal Phoenix derelict. Tourists swarm in the hotel:
the Hurlers halt. Welcome to Minions.
Caradon Hill transmitter buzzes on the other side
of the grey moor. Television signals, fog-lamps, fly-
  struck red.

Jack Wolf

Behemot

We walk – the boy and I – up to King Arthur's Hall,
Over Ladydown from Penvorder
In the mist. The footpath takes us through the
  scattered gorse,
Sheep-haunted yellow flowers, shivering on
Through enclosed fields, and onto cattle land.

They are hardy breeds: Highlands and Belted
  Galloways,
Long horned, tough coated, modern Aurochs
Staring off into the distance, stamping bullish feet,
Imprinting letter Bs into the smooth earth, breathing
  clouds.
And we – the boy and I – we walk,

Maintaining a respectful space between ourselves
And these, a space that whispers
Behemot – the Hebrew word for creatures:
bet hey mem vav tau, five letters brought to life
By vagrant breath, *ruach* sown through sky.

They turn their heads, heavy as boulders, as we walk
Watching us, through damp light, as we walk
Across a mat of sheep's fescue, heath's bedstraw,
  common bent,
Up to the foresters' stockade, up to
King Arthur's Hall, the place of sanctuary.

Dog Walking Weather

Six hundred years ago, they say – that is, five clear-cut
Centuries before the trees came down
To feed the smelting furnaces and power the beams,
This mist-lit marsh was thronged with *behemot*:
Brown bear, wild boar, elk, lynx.

So the cow-herds commandeered
This rectangle of ancient stones, this mortuary ground,
And built on it a pound to muster strays, complete with ten-foot palisade
Of wood and daub, thrown up on steep stone banks;
Set fire to frighten the night-wolves,

The wanderers. Now, just the half-tamed cattle are kept out.
Un-grazed, the heather sprouts bright crimson from the banks.
White cottongrass quickens the bog beneath.
We stay – the boy and I – we stay
Just long enough to hear the silence breathing.

Jack Wolf

Proustian Heifers

I met the heifers in the field, two hundred yards
  behind the house.
Young Belgian heifers, ginger, brindled, black, as
  curious and dangerous as kittens.
They didn't stand still staring, stamp the frigid
  ground like native cattle do,
Hooves harder than clock bells, a double warning.
They began to crowd around me, three deep, four
  deep, six.

They were two dozen overall. Two dozen young
  beef heifers, vibrantly alive,
Pressed shoulder against shoulder in a Cornish field,
  snorting fragrant steam.
They crowded in a circle, watching me through dark
  lashed eyes
That seemed too knowing, like the eyes of brides. I
  tried to walk away, but they
Began to follow me at an unsteady distance, still too
  close, too close

And all at once I caught the madeleine stench
Of mud-plastered warm heifers: ripe and sour and
  raw imprint
Of everything that ever was and never was. I was
  afraid of them. I stamped
My walking stick upon the brittle grass, and then the
  heifers scattered,
Like moments of a lost love, out of place, out of
  time.

Dog Walking Weather

Fragments

                                                A speck of
memory
                                                       gritty
between my teeth

                                              like unwashed
spinach
                                             or a fragment of
eggshell.

                                            In the storm racked
blackthorn tree,
                                                  the wren's
still singing.

                                                       Seems
the blasted slopes
                                            of this high moor
are kinder than our hearts.

Jack Wolf

Wire

My little white spaniel bitch
is chasing partridge chicks

a freed electron whizzing over the grazed field
right up to the sheep wire which stops her dead

but they slip through, dark matter
in the grey green of the keeper's covet.

So frantically she spins
and whirls and whines

black wet nose snuffling,
yelping in outraged surprise

that such an insubstantial stoppage could suspend
such animated, unrestrained delight.

Dog Walking Weather

Of Rats and Men

i)
I think I ran over a rat
while driving down the dark back lane last night

I think I saw it run beneath my wheels
it ran out underneath my wheels

a sudden black flash of wild rat
wild vanishing beneath my wheels

who would stop
for a rat? I could

not stop I had no time to stop
didn't dare didn't stop didn't

ii)
A mate phones to say he's got trouble with mice
while I am googling ways to get a bloodstain out
of concrete. It's pretty big, the stain,
and it's been there three days,
and every time I look at it I think of how it got there.

I tell him how I lived with mice once, in a place
I rented when the boy was just a baby.
1720 AD, something like that: old and crumbly,
hollow plaster walls. The mice
went scritter scratching every night,
a rain of murine footsteps on the ceiling,
rustlings in the pantry, little whiskery faces
peeping at me over cupboard tops.
Thought they were rats at first. I trapped

one with milk chocolate, put it carefully outside.
A few months later, I took in a rescue cat.
The mice all vanished. Moved out, hopefully.
I don't want to believe that they fell prey
to someone bigger, nastier – especially when
I'd only homed the cat because like me
the poor thing was a trauma case.

I tell him how a few years after this, my brother,
not to be outdone, had rats behind the dishwasher
and in the garden shed. He caught one hiding
on the low shelf where they kept the welly boots,
looking for the world like nothing worse
than mouse, until it leapt

and then it seemed to stretch, and kept on stretching.

Brother used a glue trap in the end, despatched it
with a brick. Blood everywhere. Suppose
that was a mercy, of a sort.

Google tells me that dilute ammonia, soapy water,
sand, bicarbonate of soda, household bleach
are all effective on small stains: but
they won't touch
the black clots of last Sunday's stabbing,
bubbling the stone-faced breeze-block wall
that saved his life, held up his punctured
femoral higher than his head. Seems some of us
get lucky, though we'd never know it.

I tell my mate he's got it sweet: he knows
his mice are nothing more and nothing less than
mice; while other men get mice mixed up with rats,
and rats with men.

iii)
But the future belongs to rats, not men.
Rats are small, smart, fast and furry
and almost have opposable thumbs.
They breed like rats, exponentially,
hovering in the cracks, surviving
nuclear war, starvation, and pneumonic plague.

Someday very soon, this planet's parquet floor
will be all covered by a seething rug of rats.
Rats will be everywhere.
Rats dripping down the mossy drainpipes.
Rats chewing through charred doors.
Rats pulling mouldy stuffing
from half-rotted mattresses
and splintered sofas in the places
where the men lived, for a time,
before the walls went up, before
the world fell down.

Men should celebrate rats.
Rats who keep on keeping on, despite
their lack of colour vision, and
their scrabbling claws,
their bare-arsed cheek,
their naked, insufferable tails.

Jack Wolf

Rough Tor, with Waterloo and Sheep

Heading east from Camelford I pull in on a pang
at the side of the road, onto a weathered slough
of red sand and white gravel dotted with dry dung.
In the near southern distance sits Rough Tor -
that peraluminous two-mica bubble that up-splurged
from earth's hot heart sometime during the Permian,
appearing at the surface like some ancient temple
that stood unmolested for a thousand years, before
being shattered by one month of war,
its altars once held sacred now profaned
by ignorance, the wilful disillusionment of land
stripped of all meaning. This morning, I was reading
how, sometime long after Waterloo, a Cornishman
who had served under Wellington
remarked in horrified disgust that the blue
corpses of dead men defiled upon the stones
of old Napoleon's ambition put him back in mind
of these strewn rocks surrounding bloody old Rough
Tor, for him forever crowning this part of the moor
a second La Haye Sainte. That little farm
was never a temple, its only altars those erected to
the small comforts of peaceful things: a drystone
  barn; a rusted plough; a well.
Sheep graze today over the flatlands on this north
face of Rough Tor, just as they did upon that soon
-to-be contested Belgian scarp
on the 18th of June, 1815. From morning clouds
now echoes an alarm of clashing blades:
a Royal Air Force helicopter, heading in
towards Davidstow Airfield landing strip.

Accidental Blue

Today the sky is silver grey velour
                         and silver light streaming
brilliant onto garage roofs
                         through the pale silvery wash
of autumn morning fog that floats
                         upon the dark grey-green horizon.

Over my house edgeless clouds
                 melt into silver vapour and then coalesce
again around particulate fingerprints
                 of sun-wheeled coal and microscopic
hexagons of silvery water ice.

Always hexagons, because
                       the water molecule, my love,
(quite unlike me, or you)
                       always bonds in the same way,
despite the inherent instability
                       of cloud formations in a silver sky
that flickers unexpectedly
                             an accidental blue.

Jack Wolf

Deviock Cross

Yesterday, some distance east of Lidcutt
Woods, we stumbled, unexpectedly, on
the carved wheel-head and the grooved tapering
shaft of Deviock Cross, unbroken by
five centuries of weathering and war.
It was a travellers' cross, once - a waymark
upon the faint track that then led towards
St Mary's Chapel from beyond Treslea -
skirting the fortress land, the ghost-moor, un-
crossed miles of misremembered black peat bogs,
rough forest, heathered tors, a heathen wind.
Monks and pilgrims rising in donkey-carts
from the tamed valley would have seen it, and
given thanks for being thus far delivered,
thus far saved from devils and the sins of
human hearts, before scrambling down to hood
their frightened souls in pious penitence.

Today, Chapel and track are gone: only
the granite cross remains. More wheels have turned.
Driving to Bodmin in Bank Holiday rain,
I speed on through a flatland of ideas
across a map where only distance matters,
pinked by no holy punctums, no waymarks.
The stone stands distant from the metalled road,
beyond, the fearsome moorland sprites, the wild
unpeopled edges of the world, have worn
and weathered away. In the commercial
larch woods under Deviock, the columned
trees grow fast. The path beside Cardinham

Dog Walking Weather

Water's crammed with parents pushing prams and
loping long-legged dogs. Off-road cyclists whizz
along narrow trails, thrill-chasing pilgrims
seeking only momentarily to be
reminded of the fact that there is still
something instead of nothing, road and cut-
stone circumstance.
                      In Wood's Cafe garden,
the well-fed tabby dreams of sparrows, all
quiet in the shadow of a Buddah's head.

Jack Wolf

Woodpeckers

Early March's unexpected blizzard
Blew a woodpecker onto my garden feeder.
Black-headed, ruby-arsed against the glare
Of eastern snow, she clung on, taking on
All comers, scaring the buff yellow pants
Off the great tits and tough nuthatches
Who'd all owned the gaff right up till then,
Throwing the poor chiff-chaff who'd just flown
A thousand miles to flop inside my gate
Into a funk. I named her for the storm.

When I was four some bigger kids at school
Had a nick-name for me: '*Woodpecker.*' Dead-name
Rhyme. Names quickly spun to knee-strikes. *'Let
them work it all out by themselves.'* Years later
I learned this mob anarchy of children let
To get out of control, play-acting primate politics
On asphalt, working out
Only that Might makes Right, and Power
Is the rock thrown by the biggest tossers
Had all been some mad idea of the headmaster's.

Winter redux brings the smells
Of paraffin oil, coal smoke, wood-ash deep
Within the fire pan. Comforts, though I do regret
The carbon. All the shops are closed. No-one can get
To work. I bake bread, seal the knackered oven
With a whipped towel to preserve the heat.
Outside, Woodpecker lords the feeder. How I wish
I'd had the spunk to lord the playground, put

Dog Walking Weather

The monkey bullies in their place.
It really was a matter of life and death, though

No-one understood that at the time.
The consequences wouldn't show till later.
Children don't bounce back, whatever old
Headmasters say: adults re-moult the plumage
Of their infancy. I envy this Woodpecker.
She so wants to live. I only wish
I wanted it as much: wish I could peck
Some long-deserved holes in a few thick skulls,
Pin up my primary feathers in blood red and black,
The warning colours of trouble instead of silent
   white.

You city people misperceive the country, fail to see
Its bleakness, blinded by its beauty. In the council
Cottage where my step-grandparents dragged up
Fifteen tinker kids, a broken gun
Stood propped below the stairs. For potting rabbits.
'And', they said, *'he beats her'*. Fourteen and
Already fucked, my brother tucked
A flick-knife in his blazer pocket. It saw action, too,
During that long bright summer when the wheat
Stood ripe, the hedges snied with elderberries

And chimpanzees. The cut was only superficial,
But it did the trick. No fucker said a word.
No fucker wanted to admit
A besting by the raggle-taggle. This weird year
The ploughed fields right behind my house
Lie muffled under snowdrifts. No songbirds
Are singing in the wood, the new-bud trees all

Jack Wolf

Strung out by the cold: spring rendered speechless
By the winter's shock arrival three months late.
Ice flowers are ripening into woodpeckers.
Cold's brought a reckoning, red and black.

Dog Walking Weather

Pink Sheep

Taking the bend at sixty miles an hour
I caught sight of them through the ragged hedge.
Pink sheep! Pink sheep! Shocking bright pink sheep!

Pink like the ride-on seats of a deserted roundabout
Left standing in an empty field, reflecting the last rays
Of Autumn sunset. Pink like plastic flamingos, prancing elephants.
And in that pinked out instant of astonishment I could not be quite sure
Whether the sheep were really pink, or I was only seeing pink:
Clown-pink, punk-rock pink, pretty pink, seeing
Pink instead of red:

But speeding along at sixty miles an hour, taking
A dangerous bend somewhere smack in the middle
Of this cold deserted moor I couldn't

Rubber my pink neck and look back, to make sure
Of what I really saw from what I did not see, what really happened
From what never did. I didn't want to crash
The damned car, after all, despite appearances. In hindsight now
It doesn't seem to matter much. Pink is as pink does.

I think I will be happier than I was.

Jack Wolf

Army Manoeuvres

Hear that?

                                                  What?

That rumbling. Can you hear it? You know what that is? Army manoeuvres. That's the British army practising on Salisbury Plain.

                Salisbury Plain? That's miles away.
Fifty at least. Bloody hell. Is that really what it is?

I hear it a lot. Used to hear it booming through the window, and think, is it thunder? Can't be, sky's as clear as a bell. Shockwave makes the walls shake, sometimes.

> *I think about the First World War. The big guns echoing, the shockwaves travelling.*
>
> *A hundred years on, they're still going:*
> *a never ending rumbling*
> *a tsunami that's still rattling*
> *the walls of Mosul and Calais,*
> *Kabul and Gravesend and old Salisbury.*

Can you hear it? You know what that is?

                Army manoeuvres. Big guns echoing.

Mont Blanc and the Virus

At first they said it was TB, now they're convinced
It's not – it's just some hard nut pathogen I picked
Up somewhere that's gotten the jump on my white cells.
And there I was daydreaming about Shelley and
Keats in Rome and writing out my epitaph:

*Here
Lies one whose name was carved
on the glacial surface
Of Mont Blanc, not writ in water.*

                                           But it seems that
I'm not going to die anytime soon, at least
As long as I stick out the tyranny of little
Pills and don't give in to the temptation to O -
Verdose on painkillers, make myself a martyr
To the Western plague. At least it looks like I've got
Something, some satisfying sickness simmering
Beneath my ribs, almost as enjoyable as
The transient ecstasy of orgasm, but not
Nearly as dangerous. I'd much rather cough than kiss
A stranger for my kicks. Can't think how normal people
Do that. Give me aseptic intercourse any
Day over the virus of intimacy – much
Too hard to scrub that bugger off, once you've caught it.
Sex only makes more trouble anyway, you know.
Seven billion and rising, oh the horror, and
The carbon footprint of the average Englishman

Jack Wolf

True born or not would take at least two planets to
Support, and everybody thinks they ought to have
The right to play at passengers on the top deck
Of the Titanic. I'd run for the lifeboats, love,
If I were you. I've seen what's coming, and it isn't
Pretty. Mont Blanc's melting, Shelley, and
The water's running cold and black with

Everybody's

Name writ in it. You realise you went and capsized
Back when the sea was fit to sink in, not chock full
Of oil and plastic rain, and rising, rising.

Lifeboats

It's thirty-three degrees today in London, so they say,
But here it's barely reached thirteen, below
These black clouds weighted down with weeks of
  rain.
Can you recall the first time we saw rain like this?
Rain hard as nails, a callous sky-river of rain
That boiled over the gutters, spilled the sewer pipes,
Swamping narrow streets beneath indifferent
  water;
Forty days and nights of solid rain, black rain, that
  changed
Meadows to cesspools, homes to prison ships. Only
The herons made it out unharmed. The rest of us
Clung shivering to upstairs window-frames
And battered roofs, waiting for boats that never
  came,
While in the sodden flatlands, new lambs drowned.

You refused to understand that this was now
The New Now, the New Normal, as they say, the
  world
As we have made it: thunderous and wrathful
As the sky over Akkad, that furious face
Beneath whose pent-up rage Noah built an ark, a
  lifeboat
To escape the breathless chaos of the waters. No.
You wanted it to be extraordinary, divine.
A one in several hundred, thousand year event, like
  the
Explosive outpouring of pumice-stone and red-hot

sulphur gas
That levelled Sodom; and for us to be its smug survivors, scarred

Only by living through an interesting time.
The second time the rain came, we were almost ready, though
In unexpected places the dark torrent reached still higher than before,
Bursting the defences we had built to channel it away.
It was dead water, stink-eye water, thick
With river mud and slurry from the upland farms:
A bitter brown flood-tide sloshing in over lime-
White window-sills and pouring in through air-bricks,
Drowning newly-fitted carpets and our freshly plastered walls.

So much for smug.
I don't know what there is that we can do,
(if there is anything at all that we can do)
That might persuade these furious skies forego this pummelling.
There seems no point in praying: words
Are meaningless against this flood, propitiations piddling.
Who now will craft for us a lifeboat, a deluge-going ark to bear us up
Beyond the reach of these insulted tides, this unforgiving warmth,
These waters without life, this loveless rain?

Dog Walking Weather

Stoney Littleton Long Barrow, at Halloween

"Do not go gently into that good night"
Dylan Thomas

A beautiful Halloween, again.
A beautiful Halloween, brilliant and mild with white
 sunshine and opalescent mist
shrouding the rooftops and the red beech trees, the
 just-mown grass still green,
still glistening with dew that's still not lifted.

Just like last year when I took out my spaniel bitch
 up over the green hill to the long barrow
the still onset of an autumn paused one foot in
 summer, one in the encroaching dark,
the pewter cold of stark November. One last day of
 warmth, one fading chance to feel
what soon would be but memory. I unclipped my
 little bitch

and we walked over through the pasturelands where
 some months earlier I'd heard
a yellowhammer's saw edged wheeze from the
 machine-hacked hedge beside the oilseed rape.
I watched a kestrel dive in scrub, then climbed the
 wooden stile, passed through the gap
into the silent oval of the past, the bone-house of
 antiquity.

And while my bitch explored the limits of the
 mound, pursued
the paw-stink tracks of fox and vole and stoat, I sat
 there in the forecourt, in the last light,
and I wondered if the men who built it cared at all

for Halloween, or if
they did not mark this moment of old summer's
  going gently into that good night.

They weren't like us, you see, those men who built
  the long barrow.
They didn't try to hide all traces of the dead, felt
  little dread of them arising
like the hard truth from the grave. To them, that
  great distinction
between death and life was softer than an eyelash,
  thinner than a breath

in time of famine. As close as love, death fell among
  them
like a friend long missed, a ghost soul singing sweet
  songs to the air.
– This might not have happened. I might have it
  wrong. It's possible
that to them, just like us, death was a wide mouthed
  monster, wild land stalking wraith

placated only by the watchful urns in the de-fleshing
  court of the long barrow,
dire force unstoppable, inevitable, and all too
  familiar. I bent beneath the capstone, crawled
inside the mound's dry chambered heart, and found
  in every niche a photograph, memento of
a loved one lost, a stranger's grief. A pretty girl just
  in her teens. A young man, dancing like a fool.

I closed my eyes, let go the guise of time, the
  centuries of stone; settled my spine
against the backbone of prehistory. I tried hard to
  convince myself that these
small offerings of printed light were just the modern

Dog Walking Weather

   versions of those fired clay urns
of charred and splintered bone that long ago were
   placed within it. But my bitch

kept snuffling round the septal, marking stark the
   new divide between the busy living
and the helpless dead; and I could not pretend I did
   not know that these un-solid fetishes would melt
into a million plastic particles, leach dyes and
   biocides into bare ground.
In this age of extinction, it seems even grief
   contaminates the earth.

I picked them up, and put them in my pocket.

The weatherman today on my TV says that
   tomorrow's temperatures will tumble, and there'll
be dense fog, the coldest day so far, first frosts of an
   approaching winter. If by some miracle
the middle of the week roars in on white winds from
   the east, it will freeze all the gutter puddles,
and coat all the crackling grass with a pale skin of
   subtle ice. Dog walking weather.

But it might not happen. Weathermen have got it
   wrong before. It may be instead
that over oceans distant from this place, the lingering
   heat will prove, as it has done
these past ten years and counting, a pied genesis of
   storms, white whirling vortices of hard black rain
that turns ploughed ground to clagging mud, washes
   away the stones of memory.

I wonder if the ones who came before us – those
   long barrow men –
I wonder if they were afraid of changes in the

weather.
I don't suppose they had the slightest clue that if the
  planet warmed, and kept on warming,
someday they might see all the whole world dead,
all poisoned, drowned beneath a toxic ocean.

I'm sure they never would have guessed how secret
  death
that burps invisible from simmering sea-brine
could take us out as easily as if we were
the worm ancestors of the dinosaurs.

It might not happen. Scientists revise predictions all
  the time.
They get things wrong, just like me and the
  weathermen. And beauty like today's
is hard to fear, its menace unimaginable. How can it
  be that there is danger here,
where kestrels hover, and the golden leaves lie
  peppering the black loam of the beech wood?

Who can say that it isn't just my curse
to think apocalyptically, to dread the utter ending of
  the world
when really this unending fall, this terrifying
  mildness
in the end may mean nought worse than just the
  ending of the world as we have made it?

No bad thing.

But when has death appeared as we've expected?
When has that imperfect instant, taloned moment,
  ancient friend
rung on the bell, entered politely and on time
  through the skull-door?

Dog Walking Weather

Never once when we've been ready, never in a form
  that we've imagined.

No strung puppet of old bones, no winter queen.
  Death these days is the CO_2 of private planes,
the spears of autumn bluebells, the unnatural
  mildness of this coming winter,
with its blue skies and its mellow damps, its grass-
  green anniversaries.
I think tomorrow, even if it does not freeze, I'll walk
  my bitch again, and we will trace

the old path through the beechwood. We'll climb up
  the valley sides, where flickering brown
hen-pheasants hunker down in the dry-rattle
  hogweed patch. I'll watch for kestrels quivering
over fields of oilseed rape. My bitch will track the
  mole-trails through the marbled grass. I'll bend
my neck again beneath the septal stone, re-tread
  small human steps into the dark.

I'll go because the sun is slanting bright, and golden
  mist is hazing the beech trees
and everything is beautiful, so beautiful despite it
  all, despite –
– I'll go because what, in the face of so much death,
can we do other than persist? What,
other than pretend, other than pray that everything
  will be all right

and that six thousand years from now there still
  will be hogweeds and kestrels,
yellowhammers and bright leafed beech woods.
What can we do but hope
that winter, when it comes, won't prove the end, but
  just a reckoning, a cut

that leaves clean bones untouched, preserved in the
communal niche of memory?

Nothing, nothing. Never give up hope, even as the
world ends. We are
all ancestors of those who come after. We must build
long barrows, cement grief
in stones, pack fear inside cremation urns, refuse
death's invitation to despair.
Dance, dance like fools. Right now we are the
living, and the day is not yet over,

and the sun is brilliant and mild, and opalescent mist
is pearling the beech trees.
Dread may still prove a cornerstone of hope.
Fight. Fight. *Rage, rage, against the dying of the
light.*
It's a beautiful Halloween. Tomorrow, I will walk
my bitch again.

Managed Retreat

This place where roots are gathered on the Arctic shore
already looks as if it could be picked up in one giant hand
and set down somewhere else. Stilt-lifted houses
built on permafrost, as temporary as a gold-rush camp,
unreachable except by four-by-four or light aircraft
crossing the trackless tundra. This impermanence
is an illusion (or it was)

Utqiagvik, this naked place of roots,
this place where snowy owls are hunted,
whalers' harbour reaching out to sea,
has stood here in some form or other for a thousand years,
the dry land only settled by permission
of the ice crusting the sea, ice locked
within the soil, ice hard as concrete, cold enough to freeze
whale meat and blubber, summer caught to last
the sixty-five nights of sunless midwinter.

Now all that lies beneath
is melting into air. Eight meters deep
below twelve thousand year old ice will not re-freeze again
for another thousand years; and that's
assuming we get lucky. Solid earth is melting into cold

brown soup, a slushing mesh of holes. A thousand years
are sinking fast, a thousand roots must be
pulled up quick from stagnating soil, gathered in
from the unfreezing tundra, one old tuber at a time.

Look! This one's shaped like a walrus;
this one's a beluga; this one's a skin boat.
And here's the blanket toss, *nalukataq*;
and here's the springtime festival, opening the seas.
Here's one that looks like Frederick Beechey, sailing down
the wind-washed strait, and wishing in his English heart
that this blood-curdling, bone-crack Arctic cold
would by some righteous miracle
begin to warm, and that the frozen ground
would soften. What's happened since... well

I suppose it's not all Beechey's fault. This land of roots and owls
has always been the shoreline, fragile glass frontier
of human history. Life here cannot persist
without the old permissive paradox of its deep ice:
without the dark platform. And so now must begin
the landward exile; trail of tears; managed retreat.
Pick up the wooden houses, one by one. Pack up the future on the back of a dog-sled
and pull it who knows where through the fast-thawing slush.
Do not forget to gather roots.
If nothing else, you must make time for this.

Dog Walking Weather

Equinoctial Horses

Seven days after the World Wide Web went down
One last time, and the airwaves fell as silent as the
  past,
They manifested out of nowhere, in the stubble field
Beneath the mobile mast. Four horses.
Lame, exhausted, broken-winded things:
The four sway-backed old nags of the Apocalypse.
We didn't know what to do with them. We had
No stabling left, no paddocks, nowhere
We might sensibly pasture four dying horses.
We discussed getting the shotgun. But then
Where and how ought we to have concealed
The carcasses of four apocalyptic steeds?
In the end we did nothing at all. We left
The gate wide open and the stubble unploughed.
It was the twenty-second of September.

The next day was the first, and after that the
  lengthening
Nights brought on the pains of winter, sloshing rains
And sleet that turned the world to mire. The horses
Stayed right where we'd found them, shoeless in the
  mud,
Ignored the open gate, the road beyond. Each day we
Struggled through the barren clag to see if they had
  gone,
But they had claimed the field; it soon began to seem
As if the soil answered to them instead of us.
Somebody said we ought to chase them out, but
Nobody dared be the one to do it, so the change

Jack Wolf

Became a steady state, established and
    incontrovertible.
After a while our interest in them waned, and
We stopped going out to check. We just assumed
They were still there: four horses inconveniently
    manifested
Out of nowhere. Mid-November

The old mobile mast began to rust. We were
    surprised,
Because the mast had always seemed to us
Invincible. We went back into the field, we circled
    round it,
While the horses stood foursquare, watching us
Out of half-blind sunken eyes as we danced round
And round the rotting metal. We could not tell at all
What they were thinking. One of them
Was chestnut red, tall as a warhorse and his flanks
Flecked with white hairs where spurs had dug
Into his sides: the unmistakable scars
Of appalling horsemanship. We imagined
We could see old battles playing
In his eyes, their liquid sheen reflecting
Back to us a sort of Armistice.
We thought about the shotgun, but again

None of us dared to fetch it. By Midwinter, the mast
Had fallen down. But still the horses stayed,
Inevitable, inexplicable. When we went back
In February to re-seed the field, we could no longer
    tell
It from the wilderness: only the steel gate left open
To the road reminded us where it had been. If

Dog Walking Weather

The four horses were still there they were too well
　concealed
Behind the thickening alder and young willow scrub
For us to see them. We did not try enter,
Dragged our plough home, left the land alone to its
New masters. It seemed only right. By May,
Even the gate had rusted off its hinges,
Brambles growing chest high between the posts.
We nipped the young buds off the hawthorn boughs,
Picked garlic mustard, nettles, horse mushrooms.

Seemed only right. The light came back as spring
Expanded into summer. We stopped asking one
　another where
The world had gone: the Web, the mast, the gate.
Forgot the shotgun. We'd no bullets left now
Anyway, nor skill or means of making any more.
We left it broken by the far wall, propped up on
An empty crate that had been used for apples. By
Midsummer, the gun had disappeared. We knew
This was a good thing. One day, we thought
We heard hooves coming closer, thought
We saw the horses walking slowly down the lane.
The red was leading, three greys shuffling behind:
Sway-backed, lame, exhausted, broken winded
Things. We didn't dare to blink in case we missed
　them.
Afterwards, we couldn't be sure they'd been there at
all.

Autumn brought other worries: wild October winds
Heralded flooding, the cold Spring had
Choked the apple crop. We kept a close eye on

Jack Wolf

Our stacked supplies of firewood, cut
Into our cords of oak and blighted ash,
Still good enough to burn, if not to sell.
It made no odds: no-one'd had any money since
The day the air fell silent. The leaves lay where they'd dropped
Along the lane. The brambles in the empty gateway
Thronged with fieldfares. Day came we ran out of matches,
But at least by then we'd relearned the old ways
Of flint and tinder. We set snares in the hedgerows.
Wild rabbits found their ways into our gardens
And our cooking pots. We started making plans.
We wove a white bowl out of willow stems. We gathered.

Dog Walking Weather

Everything is Connected to Everybody Else

Despite everyone's best efforts
(and their worst)

there is a deeper web
connecting everything that lives

and much that most would say does not.

It is still there despite

the way my mother took a broom and tried
to knock down all the cobwebs
that were lurking in the undercroft

(the dark entangling things)

and still despite
that moment years ago
when someone else – not you
stood where I stand now on this strand-line, listening

while millions of bubbles pinged
in weakening waves
and somewhere
in the distance, out of sight,
a man in a grey suit proclaimed the end of history.

The current here is depositional, leaving behind
a pebbled beach, a littoral strip
of red-brown fly-sand webbed between

the dropped rocks and the sea.
The line is not foot-friendly, being filled
with razor shells and sea-glass, but it's warm

and barefoot I walk gingerly upon
ground sandstone and grey granite from along the
   coast
black-fly-ash-fly-black particles
enmeshed by water, bound by waves.

Time could be both a particle and wave, I think.
Like light. Like space. Like everything.

Driving down today towards this coast
I passed the point where a few months ago I missed
my brother who had stopped here to assist
at a car crash. Travelling

on the same road, at the same time, quite by chance,
   he and I
happened both to be (almost) in identical location
   when the car flipped over,
skidded on its side, sending up a cloud

of fly wave dust. He was on his way
to a recording session, amps stacked in the far back
   of the van
and singer in the front seat. In her day job she
   worked
for the Avon and Somerset Police. Within seconds

she'd secured the scene, called for support, alerted
Road Traffic Control and summoned up an

Dog Walking Weather

   ambulance.
Strange chance, that saves a stranger's life. Strange
chance that I should witness, driving
right on past the scene and thinking

that could / that could never
have been me.

Today, while I was driving, stopped short at a red,
you were out, walking.
Somewhere, somewhere,
quietly just walking
onward through the limestone uplands
and fly-sand carved valleys of this seabed county.
Step by step leaving
dusty imprints all along the hollow ways
and tunnelling between hogweeds bubbly with
snails and tangling spiderwebs.
Green light. I hit the gas, you stopped dead
at a stile. Somewhere in that fly-webbed sea
the patterns shifted, old waves finally letting fall
cold sediment they'd gripped for centuries, casting
the black sand shoreward,
building up the strand-line, quietly.

Sea, car, dust, chance and all of us

and you and me entangled

still entangled, still
travelling parallel
here and here on fly-dust-silver threads.

Jack Wolf

There is no there.

There is
only the spiderweb,
the particle, the light.

Only the tide,
the sand, the wave.

Dog Walking Weather

Gnats Uprising in February

The gnats are rising up
against the pale pink salmon sky.
A gnatty revolution, falling, rising,
each grey spray scintilla
rising up

to reach the sky, the sky, the *sky*

before

dropping,
balling, one vast roiling
gnat-fall churning on
over the gravelled gulch
between the spruces and the spume
of fluffy old man's beard,

gnats falling and then rising *up*

then
falling
back
exhausted
and alone
only to rise, and rise, and *rise*

And rise

despite

Jack Wolf

Hineni

Now I am at the place

And whitebeam fluttering in the hedge
And grey bark rough leaf elms
And leathery green field maples

I am here now at the gravel place

And dark grey cool damp tart crunch dust sharp
  angle stones
And wild track snaking between hedges between
Fall red-berried hawthorns and smooth white-
trunked ash

And I am here now at the chalk stone edge,
Tilled field, time strata, fossil sea

Here is where moment is
Here is the moment

Here is   *I am I*

Voice air, splash rain,
Crunch stone, rush cloud,
Rasp elm, leaf flutter

I am at the place

Now I am at the place

The bush is burning

Thanks to everyone who has taken the time to read or listen to my poetry, and whose responses and suggestions have helped me to improve it.

Thanks to everyone whose names I do not know: the long dead monks and pilgrims and travellers and farmers and everybody else who once peopled, and by their efforts part-way formed, this ancient, ever changing landscape.

Thanks also to everyone whose name I cannot say, because it cannot be spoken by a human tongue.

Thanks to the land itself, to its winds, its waters, and its wildernesses.